RED CREEK

Amherst Writers

& Artists

Press

RED CREEK

A Requiem

Margaret Robison

Amherst Writers & Artists Press

P.O. Box 1076, Amherst, Massachusetts 01004

ISBN 0-941895-08-4

First Edition

Designed by Barbara Werden

Printed and bound by Hamilton Newell Printing

Photograph of Jury Box: John Elkins

All other photographs courtesy of *The Cairo Messenger*

The publication of this book was made possible in part by

grants from the Massachusetts Arts Lottery as

administered by the Arts Lottery Councils of

Amherst, Greenfield, Shelburne Falls, and Buckland,

and by the generous support of Stavros.

To my sons,

John Elder Robison and
Augusten X. Burroughs.

Introduction

Red Creek is the record of a journey I took in my memory, dreams, and imagination, a journey back to Cairo, Georgia, as I knew it in the thirties, forties and fifties.

Cairo is a small, rural town, just north of Tallahassee, Florida, seventy-five miles from the Gulf of Mexico, and two hundred and thirty-five miles from Atlanta. When I was growing up there, the population must have been seven or eight thousand, and about equally divided between black and white.

I was riding out the Calvary Road west of Cairo sometime in the early fifties when I saw Red Creek in my peripheral vision. Its water was thick and muddy, the red of Georgia's red clay. I don't know what called my attention to the creek that day. I must have driven past it a number of times. But it was that time of seeing it that I remember.

As I see it in my mind now, forty years after that day, and through a mixture of memory and imagination, the creek's clay banks have widened. They have been packed smooth and hard by the bare feet and hands of children scrambling up and down them. An oak tree grows near the place where the water has deepened, and from it a heavy limb extends over the water. Someone has tied a rope to the limb, and knotted in its free end, it hangs almost to the water.

Near Calvary, there was a Swamp Creek. There was a Tired Creek. Whether or not there was a Red Creek, I don't know. Perhaps I made the name up. I only know that the image I saw in my peripheral vision on the Calvary Road that day came back to me in a dream forty years later. I called it *Red Creek*.

M. R.
Shelburne Falls, Massachusetts
April 16, 1991

*Then at two o'clock this morning the
courthouse burned down! It is a sad sight to
behold. Two tall white columns are standing
and a shell around the sides. The center
caved in and is still smoldering. Papa
practiced law there so many years that I feel
that a part of my past has gone up in smoke.
I have been putting out snapdragons
and marigolds—*

From a letter from my mother,
LOUISA LEDFORD RICHTER,
February 18, 1980

Whatever color sorrow is, or death;
whatever music waits within the silence
of a girl's becoming or a woman's looking back;
whatever the blank gray
of certain childhood days
holds in a life; it's enough to know
that flower, leaf, and stem are one,
that the spider spins her web
from leaf to leaf to leaf, that everything
is joined by light.

I

Fragrance of tea olive, mint,
water faucet dripping into the mint leaves.
Banana shrub, dust rising slowly. Smell
from the stems of fresh-cut chrysanthemums.
Soft white gardenias, leaves
a deeper green than anybody's eyes.
Curious blend
at once nostalgic and funereal.

A room
that's been closed up too long and from its books
the musty smell of thousands of past rainy, humid
nights and days. Sweet powders in the bath.
Perfumes: My Sin, White Shoulders, satin bags
of pink sachets tucked into bureau drawers.

The rank smell of the pickle plant
that settles over town
while black men stand in backs of trucks
pitching shovelfuls of salt
into pickle vats. A bubbling
batch of turnip greens with fatback.

3

Corn bread baking. Spit
and sizzle of salt fish, fish roe, hoecakes.
A wet dog's strong smell as he shakes
creek water off himself.

An oyster stew.
A kitchen table set with bowls, spoons,
soda crackers, milk. Linoleum
floor buckled
from water seeping under it for years.
"And did you really find a pearl one time?"
A boy in white pajamas
poking at an oyster's lacy edge.

Smell of white sheets hanging
in the clean air of a summer afternoon.
And bed sheets tangled
in a bed not made all week.
Semen. Sweat.
Sour milk and pablum spit up
on a baby's soft knit gown. And leather
of a scuffed football, the new
cut grass. The pine tree's smell. Light
smell of ripening pears, and pears
worm-eaten, rotting on the ground,
brown speckled skin gone soft against the flesh.

Old Doctor Watson's strong cigar and those

mysterious medicinal aromas from his shelves.
Stethoscope hung from his thick neck to tell you
he knows things about the human heart
that you don't know.

And one sad afternoon across
from Roland's Auto Parts
the smell of blood that ran
sluggishly into the gutter on the sun-baked road.
A woman's cries: "He darted out!
My Lord, he's just a boy." Burnt rubber, thin
bike tires twisted like a snake.

A long time past.
Yet in my nostrils still, and stronger now, aged
mingling like a fine, full-bodied wine.
"Take, drink, this is my blood," the stained-
glass Christ kneeling
in Gethsemane. Miss Tessie Dodge
also praying, her hair frizzed and dyed
the red of Moses' burning bush.

Fragile smells. The damp
and tender top of a new baby's head.
"Be careful, now. He's new."
Bill Watson's voice:
"Who would have thought Tom Conway's blood
and brain and bone

could go so deep? His mama painted that wall twice
and still the blood shows through.
A double-barreled shotgun! Jesus Christ!"

Hay. Peanuts piled high in the barn, smells
of the chicken yard, the pigpen, warm
milk sloshing in the pail.
Old-fashioned roses. Watermelon rind.

The sweet
breath of two sisters whispering in bed,
toes touching and their flannel
gowns tangled at their knees. "Sissy,
does it hurt to die?" The ringed moon
balanced on a pittosporum bush outside
their window, dark
leaves pressed against the pane.

Scorched smell
of school clothes hung by the fire to dry.
Oiled floors in Northside Grammar School.
Chalk dust. The smell
of penny candies and coppery smell of pennies.

"Isn't it a shame, Louise?
Him so young, leaving

that nice wife and those sweet girls." The coffin
trembling when the widow kissed its lid, and rain
beat on the canvas, ran
like rivers to the grave.
"How could a just God—"
"But you know he was a drinking man."
"But how could any loving—"
"Shh, daughter, it's a sin to question God."

And I was quiet. But questioning.
I questioned eyes
of grocers, bankers, preachers.
Children on trapeze bars.
The town tramp's eyes. The barber's. Grinning eyes
of teen-age boys behind the rims of beer cans.
Eyes of teachers—white-haired Mrs. Weathers saying:
"The way a person folds a paper tells
so much about that person's character."

Grandmother's eyes. Mother's. Cousins'.
And my crippled sister's eyes. Eyes
of the mailman striding up our walk. My
father's eyes through cigarette smoke: "I'd walk
a mile for a Camel." "Call
for Phillip Morris." Luckies. "Don't,"
my father said, "look a colored boy in the eyes."
Colored boys' eyes.

"People are such damn fools."
Mack Crawford's voice.
He spits into a battered brass spittoon
and scratches the red stubble on his chin, and waits
outside the courtroom on a bench. "You think
I got the money for a fancy lawyer?
I'm lost before I walk into that room. There ain't
no justice for the poor. And you tell me
the law is just? I'll tell you
laws can kill a man." Bravura going hollow
at the gavel's sound and no more potent
than his spittle in the pot.
"But Christ's spit healed the blind."
"It's power and money make the man," Mack snorts.
Hikes his dungarees up, wipes his mouth
and rubs the back of his rough hand against his pants.

Across the street the Post Office,
its mural painted during Roosevelt's New Deal:
black men and women bending
in a field of cotton. Rows
of boxes for the mail:
bills, wedding invitations, colored
postcards from Miami Beach, Tuscaloosa,
Birmingham and Kansas City. Roanoke. A letter
from a soldier somewhere off the coast of France.

A letter saying:
"Sue died in her sleep last Monday night."
A secret-code spy ring
for two box tops from Kellogg's Cornflakes.
Six packages of seeds from Burpee's. A contract
from some northern garment factory.
Invoices. Magazines.
The *Cairo Messenger*: "Greatest
Diversified Farming Section in America."
Single copies, 5 cents. Tax
returns. And hopes
beyond this town. And dreams.
A timid girl with soft down on her sun-browned legs
slips a perfumed letter through the letter slot.
Tom Wilbur slits a letter open with his pocketknife
and puts his glasses on. Outside
the flag is flying at half-mast
but I don't know who died and no one seems to care.

Six burly men are ripping up a section of the street.
Pickaxes split the pavement and the town clock strikes.
Upstairs above the firehouse, the librarian
slips *Hedda Gabler* on a top shelf, stops
to secure a hairpin in her fine auburn hair.
She blinks her small, dark eyes

and rubber-stamps the dates
in *Wuthering Heights*.

The clock tower's four white faces compass true:
North South East West. Wood-shingled dome atop
the red brick courthouse. Hour hand
fallen from the western face. 8:42.

Clare Winslow's kitchen sink
is filled with fresh-cut roses, stems
plunged into icy water. Clare snaps
thorns off, stands each perfect bud
upright in a cut-glass vase.
Her doorbell rings. She walks
to answer it, her living room dark, its shades
still drawn against the day, the metronome
on the piano polished like a gem. She turns
the brass doorknob, and smiles:
"You should have used the service entrance, boy."

Down South Broad Street by the Wallace Simmons place
old Velma Drew on her slow weekly walk
across town to the cemetery out
past Mixon's Feed Mill and across
from Roddenbery's pickle plant. She wears
a straw hat, purple dress, and leans
on her polished cane. All morning

she'll sit by her dead husband's grave
and read the *Cairo Messenger* aloud.
"It was the highlight of dear Julian's week,"
she'll say. "It's the very least that I can do."

Look how she leans so on her cane, and drags her foot.
She'll be dead in six weeks, her supper dishes
standing in the sink, one black satin slipper
fallen from her foot.
When the milkman comes early the next morning
he won't find a bottle standing by the door, or her note:
"A pint of cream and half a pound of butter, Roger.
Have a good day. Velma Drew."

In Wilson Hardware, Sue Smith
dusts rows of crystal while Will Maxwell
unpacks a new order of heavy duty pliers.
Up front a sharp ring, and the cash drawer slams.
Someone has bought a key chain and a small Yale lock.
Sue wipes dead flies to the floor and props
a cardboard sign by Haviland's Gold Band.
"Marjorie Weatherbury's Choice."
And in small letters underneath, a list
of patterns for the bride's silver and crystal.
Around the card, a border of forget-me-nots
Sue painted last night with her water-color set.

At McCrory's, Macy Beauford
has just shoplifted two lipsticks, a box
of Maybelline mascara.
She wears a bright
flowered dress hung loosely from
broad, bony shoulders, waist
gathered with a rhinestone-studded belt.
She runs her tongue across her teeth and smiles:
"Give me a bag of popcorn, honey,
and a quarter pound of them
dark chocolate cream drops with the cherry centers."

I hear the sound of hammering
from the Shoe Shop, slap
of cloth on leather, three
young bankers walk into the Citizen's Cafe.
Jake Poller grinds his storefront awning down.

Across the street from Mizell's Drugs
someone is sweeping
the train-station loading platform.
By the track
a steamer trunk and two
suitcases, a woman
in a wide-brimmed hat and straight long skirt,
a woman from another time, or image
from a dream.

I wipe my eyes as if to wipe
the bright late-morning sun away, as if
sunlight would stream like sparks
from both my fists and clear my eyes
of images that mix my memory and dreams to form
a vision I can't understand, and I
cannot console the woman as she weeps.

And why have I returned
to walk these streets?
And why am I so drawn
to study hard each face, and each
detail of this small town down to the weeds
forced up through cracks in sidewalks, light
reflected from a lost skate key
beneath a pittosporum bush?

Childhood is gone. And youth. And ties
with people I have loved
are broken now. My grief is more than I
can easily contain. My grief
builds this town anew and raises all the dead
to walk this day with me. And I

don't know the month or year, the scents
of flowers from all seasons rise

to fill the air and I
can turn a corner where a wind waits chill as winter
and I think
that I remember

men in dark suits and black derby hats,
their silhouettes precise
against the river's midday glare of sun, the long
deep lawn of coarse grass spreading
from the water up the hill beyond.
How slowly they ascend the hill, these men.
And in their center, hoisted high
a plain pine coffin lacquered black. But
these men are not
from my lifetime, their clothes
are those of many years before my birth, or my
dead father's birth, a time
when this town was so new dust rose
from hooves of horses and the smells
of harness leather and the sweat
from flanks of horses mixed with patent medicine
aromas and the smell of pine.

But as a child I once stood on this spot
here by the street and felt
a certain grayness of the afternoon and was
aware of courthouse, palms,
Post Office, the drab front

14

of the picture show. But not
the letters on its dull marquee, or some
new poster advertising: NEXT ATTRACTION. Nothing
but the buildings' shapes, long
shadows and the glare
of sunlight bleaching shapes almost to air.

I watched
a small plane move so slowly from the east to west
I half-expected it to fall
like ash
from leaves that burned
in piles along South Broad Street in the fall.
Or like
a feather, delicate
as spider webs
among the leaves of a gardenia.

═══════════════════════

II

A wind is rising now, the tail end
of a hurricane that spends its fury
somewhere off the coast.
The smell of rain is in the air and pine
trees now begin
their slow rock rocking and I think

I hear the sharp crack of a limb and a low
distant sound that could be thunder.

Look how dark the sky has grown and how
that large bird cries
as it circles over town. And in
Clint Bell's cow pasture, a young calf
with a broken leg
struggles to stand up and cannot.

The late afternoon of the approaching storm
was darker than most nights.
All evening long I hear
static on the radios and

somewhere
on a phonograph
Caruso sings.

Everything is dark
except the headlights
from a car
that drives through on its way to Key West,
insects plastered on the headlights' domes of glass.
A moth with one wing torn by wind.

Now all the town's asleep.
I wander. Wind
sweeps the street and sidewalks clean,
crushed papers blown against the curb
and spinning. Storefronts
tightly shut.

One paper caught and fluttering
between the bars
of a black picket fence. A limb
that knocks against an attic window.

The Mixons' monkey clutches at a branch
of the pecan tree in their yard and lays his head
against the rough bark. His eyes
are opened wide.

At Mary Richards', wind
through a half-opened window billows
the silk draperies
across the living room almost to touch
the grand piano that no one has played in years
while Mary sleeps
beneath a satin quilt stained brown
from coffee spills, and burned
from cigarettes.
The day her daughter dies of sleeping pills, she'll hang
a black wreath on her door and paint a sign:
NO VISITORS
Tonight she sleeps a dreamless sleep.

The hinges on a chicken coop
are creaking but the hens
are undisturbed while the white rooster
lifts his wings an instant
and ruffles the fine feathers on his neck.

In the field near Northside Grammar School
sandspurs tangle in the wind to knots of burrs.
And in the Bells' side yard a large camellia bush
shivers like a person sometimes does in sleep.

Pam Stevens' music box has just run down
for the fifth time. In the dark she reaches
to the bedside table, winds it once again.

"Dance, ballerina, dance," it plays
and on its top
a tiny ballerina spins.

Charles Wight has waked with a hoarse, hacking cough.
"You all right?" his wife asks. Charles
clears his throat. "Wind must have waked me.
Or that dream.
I was a boy again, Irene.
Imagine after all these years.
Something strange about it though.
I can't quite remember."

"Dreams don't mean a thing.
Go back to sleep."

"But there was something strange, Irene."

In a trailer on the edge of town
a Gypsy rouses from dreaming.
"There are signs," she whispers to no one.
"A rusted bucket filled with rain.
A stone fallen." She turns in bed
sleeping, a jangle
of fine silver bracelets on her wrist.

19

The wind knocks a gutter hard
against the Stevens' house and twists
the weathervane off Barry Filmore's barn.

In town, three men from that dark, mournful group
I saw ascend the hill
walk now down
the middle of the street as if
a part of some processional.
Their dark suits are identical, their hats.
I think the weather cannot touch these men.
Beside me the old
stucco hotel with dark archways
is empty. Has stood empty for years.
I walk slowly past it.

No one walks this way with me.
Even the owl sleeps. And the wren.
And I cannot see the darkness
that waits in those rooms or hear echoes
of footsteps.

I feel the air thick as water. Night air
that smells now of nothing. In the still
of this moment no leaf turns.
No memories of mine wait here.
Yet I pass this way weeping

as if the dust
were human, as if
some salesman passing through
had brought with him ash from Dachau
that had settled on the shoulders of his coat;
as if the naked bulb dangling
over the night clerk's desk
remembers still the light
of Hiroshima as it flashed.
"The bomb to put an end to war,"
my teacher said as, in the film he showed
my eighth-grade class, smoke rose
into the waiting air and spread
like history.

Now rain begins. A sudden downpour.
Lightning lights the whole town in a flash. I think
of El Greco's "Toledo"—some quality of light—
or an old photograph
one views through a stereopticon in some
old formal parlor rich with velvet and dark
polished wood.

How many of these storms I've known, how
I have loved the power of the wind. How
as a child, I stood in awe before an upturned oak,
its huge roots in the alien air. A tangle

of electric wires along the ground, the crackle
and fine sparks. No words
in any church or hallelujahs in a choir
could touch me like the wind, or rain
that runs to pool around the calf
that licks and licks its broken leg.

But once I dreamed the river bridge washed out.
And was afraid.

And if this wandering of mine is only dreaming
what difference does it make? What
difference can the dead make now,
or that I can remember
sunlight
on the folds of bed sheets one late summer morning
a whole lifetime ago?

What matters, then?
Poetry matters, and the line
that will not break
under the weight of history.
What matters then?
A single gardenia broken
from the dark-leafed bush.
What matters then?
The dark-leafed bush.
What matters then?
The gardenia.

III

To wake and see the walls becoming
fields to walk through, to wake
and see the floor becoming grass.
Sometimes the dream is more than I can hold of life.
But if I am both dream and dreamer,
I am the starless wall against the night.
I am the door through which the rivers flow.

I rest now in this broad, deep field,
the sun—red,
low in the sky, the land
turned back
to its own intentions
offering up
out of itself
the wild grasses.
Clover and black-eyed Susans.
A butterfly balanced
on a flower's thin petal.
A blackbird gliding slowly.

A scarlet tanager rising
from deep in the grasses.

In this late afternoon
sounds have lengthened
and softened. Hum
of an airplane circling. A mother
calling a child in to supper.

How the words float like echoes
that look for their source, and I think
they will always float this way, suspended.
They could be sounds from my childhood.
Or forty years past it.

From here I can see only farmland,
a field and a Gypsy's small trailer.
A row of low trees at the field's edge.
Beyond the trees Red Creek is flowing.

In dreams I've walked toward it.
My legs in the thick underbrush,
branches scratching my face.

A thin mist hangs over Red Creek.

Is it a dream of Red Creek
or a memory of drowning

that has brought me again to this town?

Or the vision
of the men who carry that black coffin
up the hill? What difference
could my presence make to them?
Or theirs to me, those men
who walked up from the river
years before my birth?

No one is drowning at Red Creek.

Only the water has risen
with last night's rainstorm, and a salamander
rests on the bank with its eyes closed.

IV

Out from town there is farmland. Fields
of squash, cucumbers, okra.
Pecan groves.
Turtles, fish, peanuts, and possums.
Cottonmouths. Rattlesnakes.

A white wood church out the Tallahassee highway
stands in an oak grove. "Come
to the church in the wildwood,"
my father sang as we passed it.
And lily-filled Lake Iamonia,
red-bellied bream in its waters.

Out the Thomasville road, the new
cemetery. The sandpit where I swam.
The Bloody Bucket Nightclub, its neon
blood drops blinking. And Cherokee
roses climbing the fences.

I feel the wind in my face.

On the roadside—a young girl carrying
a parcel, and hooked
over one thumb, the straps of her sandals.
Gloria Wilkins.

Sunday, a processional
from the Pentecostal Church on the hill
near Red Creek
will wind its way down to the water,
down the hill by the pasture
where two cows rest leaning together.
And the limb of a tree that has fallen.
They will baptize Gloria Wilkins,
long hair red as the water,
the water staining her white dress.

Parked at the edge of a gully
out the Calvary Road,
a small silver trailer on cinder blocks.
ANCIENT MYSTERIES REVEALED, the sign says
and: FORTUNES

In the yard an old Gypsy
ties bean vines
to poles, her black
head scarf a knot
at the back of her neck. She spits

in the dirt, squints her face
to the sun's glare.

Overhead a plane trails a banner:
BARNUM AND BAILEY—THE GREATEST
SHOW ON EARTH, and dates for performances.
But she does not read them. She stamps
out a hill of red ants.
And goes to the well to draw water.

What does it mean, this church
rising on a hill in my dream?
And the girl rising, too,
like grasses rise, and birds.
Like all things growing,
rooted and alive, rise.

But what are the bird's roots?
Small twigs, broken, and dried grasses.
Tangled bits of fur and hair, mud.
What the bird loved most—the nest
from which it first flew—
awkward and eager, carrying with it
the memory of the yolk of itself
round and golden like a sun.

What does it mean, this Gypsy, rising
from the palm of my open hand?
She is the mirror I polish in the night,
keeper of the keys, mother
to the woman I will become.

V

I walk home down this alley
back of the houses on North Broad,
the bamboo and the board fences dividing
white people's houses from black.

I walk through this black neighborhood
with its handful of shanties
unpainted, gray. And the yards
are gray too, hard packed and bare.

How many years has Rossie sat here
on her front porch shelling field peas?
Dust on her legs, holes cut
in her shoes for bunions—while gnats
swarm around her like the past and future, gnats
thick as the smoke that rose
the night her son Sam died
trying to rescue my uncle
from his burning house, his house burning
inside me still like history burns
when you breathe it in too deeply, too quickly.

And where is the house of the little boy who fell
from the pecan tree? "It was the fence
that killed him," Miss Mabel told me.
The black iron fence that ran along the Willard's
front yard, separating the lawn from the sidewalk.
The sidewalk where I walked, kicking
leaves in the fall.

"They always hired a little colored boy
to gather the nuts in their yard," Miss Mabel said.
"For pennies." And in my mind I saw the little boy
always barefoot and reaching. He fell
from a high branch, his chest
crashing against the fence spikes that stood
guard over the Willards' yard like an army.
His broken ribs pierced his lungs.
"It was the fence that killed him," she said,
grapes heavy on the arbor, leaves
turning on Broad Street.

At the end of the bamboo, the bamboo where
starlings roost, where rattlesnakes
sometimes wait; the bamboo over which the moon
has called and called to me; at the end of the bamboo
I enter my parents' backyard and stand here
watching Amos in the rose garden,
overalls dusted with rose poison.

He wipes his forehead, drinks
ice water from a Mason jar, and I know
almost nothing of his life,
whether he had a wife, or children.
Whether his mother loved him.

I stand here watching Amos
drinking ice water from a jar. A jar
and not a glass because he's black,
and I watch him spray the roses,
American Beauties and Peace roses,
growing there near the birdbath
where a bluejay spreads its wings,
shatters water to sparks in the sunlight
while a blackbird rises from an oak limb
and the bird dog sleeps in the bushes.

I stand here watching Amos
while on the bench by the birdbath ice melts
in the jar, droplets
of water running down its side
like tears from an ancient sorrow.

In the house I wander the rooms, touching
an unwashed cup by the kitchen sink, tracing
the back of my sister's wheelchair
with my nail-bitten thumb.

The dead are never dead, and rain
still clings to pine needles in the yard.
The sad light still falls on the living room rug
with its garden of dusty blossoms. And mother
is forever reading aloud:
"It was the best of times.
It was the worst of times." Or standing
at the back door, looking out.
My father is forever about to die, the sound
of his damaged heart filling the room
like the tick of a terrible metronome.
Or younger, healthier, he's telling my brother and me
a bedtime story of a girl and boy lost in the woods.
"Once upon a time," he begins
and the words of the story
mix in the air with the words
of my uncle's death or the news
of World War II crackling through static
on the radio or memories of my father
singing, "God Bless America"
or "When Johnny Comes Marching Home."
"Once upon a time," my father begins
and the words of the story mix
with the words of my mother's admonitions,
family arguments. The drone
of electric fans.

The dead are never dead, and my sister
is always smiling as my brother bends to kiss her, or
my sister is always having a convulsion while rain
beats on the metal awning over the terrace
where my mother has spread the winter potatoes
and a convoy of army trucks passes out front.

Or always it's late afternoon, always
it's spring. Delicate
rose-colored clouds low in the sky,
and the lonely wail of a passing train
rises to float like smoke
in the wounded air, and my father
is telling the story of the lost children
trying to find their way home.

And it is I who am haunted,
like a house is haunted.
Haunted by a history that I cannot put to rest,
haunted by the questions I still ask.
How many times have I returned
only to leave again?
There's nothing I can do here now.
Whatever the chairs remember of the days,
whatever doorknobs remember of hands,
the roof of rain,
whatever the air remembers of the silence

that choked the children's laughter,
I cannot tell these stories.
A thousand thousand words unspoken
wait in the folds of every drapery.
Words never said aloud still hide like dust
under the carpet in every room.
How can I write these stories
when the silence deafens
with its wail and roar
and echoes fill my mind
with their insistent drone
like airplanes from World War II, passing
and passing over?

The dead are never dead, and the river
never forgets the names of the drowned.
The dead are never dead, and the drowned
always remember the vowels of fishes,
the watery O that repeats and repeats itself.

This also is history—my grandmother
unpinning her long hair
and brushing and brushing it
before going to bed, the bedside lamp
casting its warm circle of light on the table.

Sometimes even the deepest silence
gathered from the days and years
expands in my chest as if to make room
for the ascending birds
when the light strikes
some simple thing—grandmother's teeth
in a cup by her bed. Or the winter potatoes
still covered with the dirt
from which my mother dug them, bending
over row after row in the Victory Garden.

VI

There is no one in town now, streets
cleared of the Saturday traffic:
Leon the truck driver.
Mildred the washwoman. Farmers.
The black pickle plant workers
who bring the smell of it with them
as if it permeated their skins. That
and the smell of popcorn
from the popcorn machine at McCrory's.
Chewing gum stuck to the sidewalk.

Only the Zebulon is open.
On its marquee: THE LONE RANGER AND TONTO.
Over the ticket window, the sign:
COLORED SEATING IN THE BALCONY.
Day gone. And early evening.
Headlights throw the cotton gin's shadow
over the train tracks. A battered
hubcap, broken
beer bottles.

Children sleep. Supper dishes
stacked in their cupboards. And someone
walks down an alleyway whistling,
"Somewhere Over the Rainbow."

A man leans on a column
on his front porch smoking a cigarette.
In his house a radio plays.
At Alonzo's gas station, a stranger
asks how many miles to Havana.

On their front porch the Massy sisters
creak in their porch swing and watch
the traffic on North Broad. A car
lights their white hair an instant.
Across the street, the Baptist
Church is dark, the stained glass
Christ gone flat
and lifeless in the night.
One sister says, "There's still a little
scuppernong jam in the pantry."
The other answers, "The hedge needs trimming
something awful, Sister."

Two cars pass
slowly. Night
lengthens. Two black cars

silent
as the darkness deepens.
The porch swing creaks.

In Booker Hill the drums are just beginning
in the black church across this town.
My own blood quickens at the sound.
I feel it throbbing
in my temples and I walk
the streets and there is nowhere
here that I can sleep. At the motel
at the edge of town NO VACANCY
shines neon red against the night.
The coffee shop is closed. The old hotel.

And I remember cries in Booker Hill.
And screams.
And someone said:
"That's just the way those niggers are.
They'd just as soon come at you
with a knife as not.
Look how they all get drunk
on Saturdays and fight
like savages. It's
all they know." The drums
beginning—

In the night,
in the purring of the tiger cat,
the train's howl,
in the overpass.
And in the sleeping owl in Barry Filmore's barn.
In every darkened room of every house.
In every tree and bush.
And in the morning glory vines. In
the Baptist Church, its stillness, dust
clinging to its rafters, in
each spiral-edged arm
of each oak pew. Between
the pages of the law books, in songs
of Gypsies camping at the edge of town.
and in the grass. Each
tree, house, stone.
Each acorn crushed on the sidewalk by someone's shoe.
and each undamaged acorn. Each
mole burrowed in the dirt, in the glint
of stars on Red Creek's water. In
all of these and above them, this:

Drumbeats from Booker Hill.
From the black church across this town.
I hear them everywhere. Insistent
like a heart, the drumhead
quivering against the drummer's hand.

And somewhere in a house near town
an ice cube clinks against a glass,
and somewhere a man asks:
"Don't the years between us matter?"

The air is thick
with honeysuckle fragrance. Magnolia
blossoms shattered on the ground.

And somewhere
on a phonograph Caruso sings.
"La commedia commedia..."
he stutters, the record needle stuck,
the record spinning

while down the street
one of the Massey sisters
has just died of a stroke, thin fingers
curling
as if to catch the late night air.

Out the Calvary Road the old Gypsy
has waked and walked barefoot
to her front door. She opens it.
Sniffs the night air.
Licks her finger
and holds it

to the wind rising now
from the gully.

A white cat stretches on a lawn.
The four clock faces on the courthouse dome
glow luminous as moons. It's time
for the late night train to Waycross.

And I stand waiting. Breathing
the night air, breathing the town.
Taking the warm air in,
releasing it. And history
is everywhere. It rises
in the dust of every dirt road in the county.
It has settled to Red Creek's bottom. It clings
to fins of fishes in the red Ochlocknee River.
It blooms on the face of the rose
and the gardenia.

Epilogue

The courthouse burned to the ground.
All four faces of the clock collapsed
into its center. The numbers. The hands.
The bell notes that struck the hours and years
still tremble in the air.
They mix with echoes
of the music of the drums
I heard as a child, drumbeats
from the black church
in Booker Hill. Drum beats
that entered the cells of my body, becoming
a part of me.

What of the tiger lily,
gold-throated and silent?
Flames of nasturtium circle the sundial.
How bright the sun is!
Look how it plays hide and seek
with that heap of broken brick
tossed there on the grass.

What was being built or torn down?
I don't know.
I only know that each
broken edge of each brick
holds the rage of any broken thing.
And words cling to the brick like sorrow
that won't let go.

There's dust everywhere.
Even the roses are dusty.
Between their petals the choked laughter
of the children waits, folded
like pages the wind does not blow away.
Even though the wind
has made the roses tremble a little
on their long green stems.
I have seen the wind
make them tremble a little

as I have heard the bell notes tremble
in the air, and my blood
remembers the black drums
as it remembers the river
in which my eyes quenched their thirst.
My blood has become that river. Even now
the ocean calls to me in my sleep.
And I have become both plowed field and melon,
sky and corn.

My legs have grown long in their dreaming.
I am at home in the roots of things.

Perhaps I imagined the town.
Or the town imagined me.
But the men in dark suits
and derby hats are real. In dreams
I have seen them ascend the hill.
Always the sky is gold.
Always the dark trees weep.

And the woman from another time
is real. Real, and inconsolable.
Mail order bride? The new school teacher?
A daughter coming home?
She stands alone with all her luggage.
And the train is gone.

What is there besides imagination
and the dust? The dust of ancestors
who still light candles for us.
So many candles.
The night sky is filled with their light.

Acknowledgments

I thank Pat Schneider who believed in *Red Creek* from its first draft, and years after that first reading searched through boxes of papers for fragments of the poem after I had almost abandoned them. Pat has made the publication of this book possible.

I thank Linda Maloney-Kohler who has believed in my poetry since I first began to write. I thank Kendall who has been able to read and hear *Red Creek* out of her own Southern beginnings. I also thank Pat Bega, Sharleen Kapp, Barbara Bosma Van Noord, Henry Lyman, Anna Kirwan Vogel, Barbara Werden, Susan Wyatt, Gene Zeiger, and Marilyn Zelwian.

Especially I want to express my gratitude to Pat. King who, in so many ways, has made my life possible.

About the Author

Margaret Robison was born in 1935 in Cairo, Georgia, and grew up there. Her first two books of poetry were *The Naked Bear* and *Here*. Before the stroke that paralyzed her left side, she taught as a Poet-in-the-Schools in Massachusetts, taught creative writing to women in prison, and served on the staff of the University of Massachusetts Summer Writing Workshop.

Margaret lives in Shelburne Falls, Massachusetts, where she is writing a book about her stroke and her recovery.